Reflections

A Child's View

Homework and Practice Book

Grade 1

Orlando Austin New York San Diego Toronto London

Visit *The Learning Site!*
www.harcourtschool.com

Printed in the United States of America

ISBN 0-15-341467-7

6 7 8 9 10 073 14 13 12 11 10 09 08 07

Reflections 

The activities in this book reinforce social studies concepts and skills in Harcourt School Publishers' ***Reflections: A Child's View***. There is one activity for each lesson and skill. In addition to activities, this book also contains reproductions of the graphic organizers that appear in the unit reviews in the Student Edition. Study guides for student reviews are also provided. Reproductions of the activity pages appear with answers in the Teacher Edition.

Contents

UNIT 3: WE LOVE OUR COUNTRY

UNIT 4: OUR CHANGING WORLD

UNIT 5: ALL ABOUT PEOPLE

UNIT 6: THE MARKETPLACE

Name ______________________ Date __________

Following Rules

Read the paragraph, and then answer the questions.

Victor's class has rules for using the computer. One rule is to finish schoolwork before using the computer. Victor did not follow this rule. The next day, he could not use the computer.

1. What rule did Victor break?

____

____

2. What happened because he broke the rule?

____

____

3. Why would it have been better for Victor to follow the rule?

____

____

CALIFORNIA STANDARDS HSS 1.1, 1.1.2

Use after reading Unit 1, Lesson 1, pages 12–15.

Name ______________________ Date ____________

CRITICAL THINKING SKILLS

Solve a Problem

Five children want to play soccer, but they cannot make two teams with the same number of players. List two ways they can solve this problem.

1 ____

2 ____

CALIFORNIA STANDARDS HSS 1.1.2

Use after reading Unit 1, Skill Lesson, pages 16–17.

Name ______________________ Date __________

Who Is Obeying the Law?

Color each person who is obeying the law.

Draw an X on each person who is not.

$50 FINE
FOR
LITTERING

CALIFORNIA STANDARDS HSS 1.1, 1.1.2

Use after reading Unit 1,
Lesson 2, pages 18–21.

Name ______________________ Date __________

Who Is the Leader?

Draw a line to match each clue with a leader. Then write the name of the leader on the line.

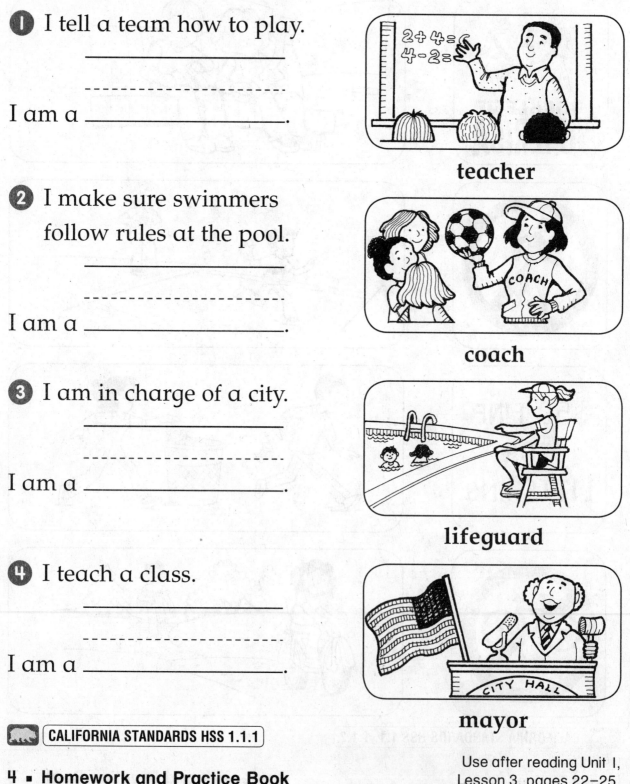

1. I tell a team how to play.

   ____

   I am a ______________________.

2. I make sure swimmers follow rules at the pool.

   ____

   I am a ______________________.

3. I am in charge of a city.

   ____

   I am a ______________________.

4. I teach a class.

   ____

   I am a ______________________.

teacher

coach

lifeguard

mayor

CALIFORNIA STANDARDS HSS 1.1.1

Use after reading Unit 1, Lesson 3, pages 22–25.

Name ______________________ Date __________

PARTICIPATION SKILLS

Make a Choice by Voting

Choose four foods, and write them on the chart. Ask children or family members to vote for their favorite food. Tally the votes on the chart. Write to tell which food wins.

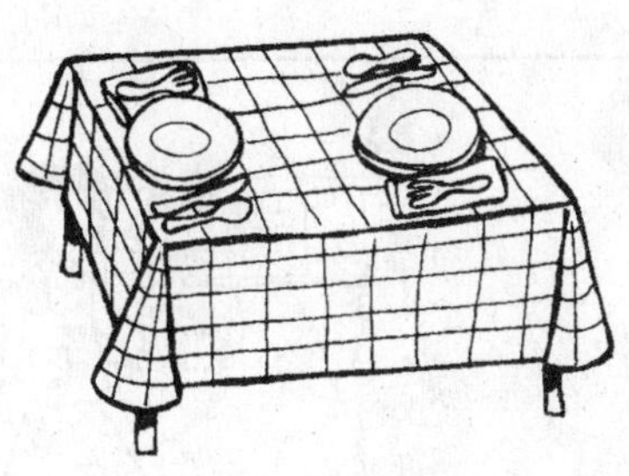

Favorite Food	Votes
1 ______________	
2 ______________	
3 ______________	
4 ______________	

5 ______________ got the most votes.

CALIFORNIA STANDARDS HSS 1.1, 1.1.1

Use after reading Unit 1, Skill Lesson, pages 26–27.

Name ____________________ Date __________

Rights and Responsibilities

Circle right or responsibility under each picture.

Go to school.

right responsibility

2

Behave and learn.

right responsibility

3

Keep your dog on a leash.

right responsibility

4

Own a pet.

right responsibility

5

Buy a car.

right responsibility

6

Obey traffic laws.

right responsibility

CALIFORNIA STANDARDS HSS 1.1, 1.1.2

Use after reading Unit 1, Lesson 4, pages 30–33.

Name ______________________ Date __________

PARTICIPATION SKILLS

Working Together

Kate, Nolan, and Ethan want to make a poster about good sportsmanship. Write what they should do to work together.

Plan together.

Act together.

Think about how well the group worked together.

 CALIFORNIA STANDARDS HSS 1.1.2; HR 2

Use after reading Unit 1, Skill Lesson, pages 34–35.

Name ______________________ Date __________

Study Guide

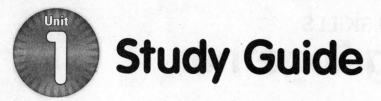

Read the paragraph. Use the words in the box to fill in the blanks.

vote	citizen	laws	leader	rules	community

People ____________ to choose the mayor. The mayor is the ____________ of our city. She helps make ____________ and ____________ to keep us safe. Everyone who lives in our ____________ must respect the laws. That is part of being a good ____________.

 CALIFORNIA STANDARDS HSS 1.1, 1.1.1, 1.1.2

Use after reading Unit 1, pages 1–48.

Name ______________________________ Date __________

READING SOCIAL STUDIES

Cause and Effect

Fill in the chart to show cause and effect.

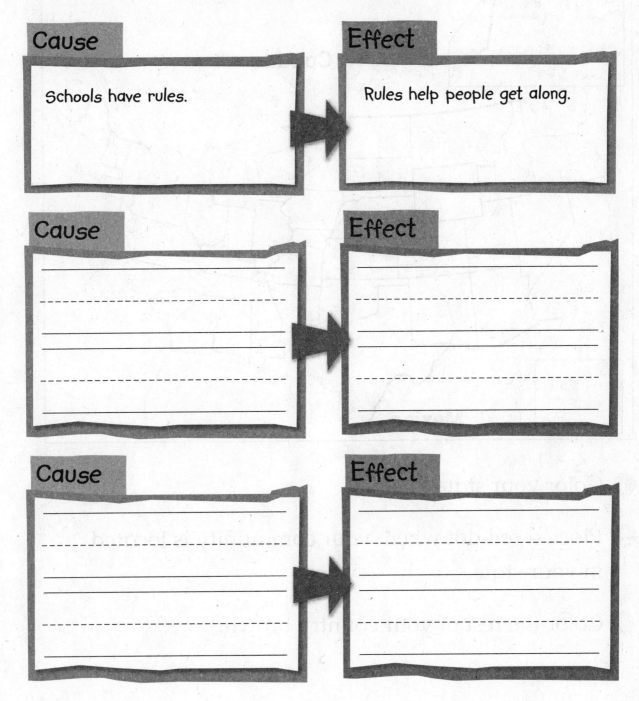

Cause	Effect
Schools have rules.	Rules help people get along.

CALIFORNIA STANDARDS HSS 1.1, 1.1.1, 1.1.2; HI 4

Use after reading Unit 1, pages 1–48.

Name ______________________ Date __________

Where You Live

Follow the directions below the map.

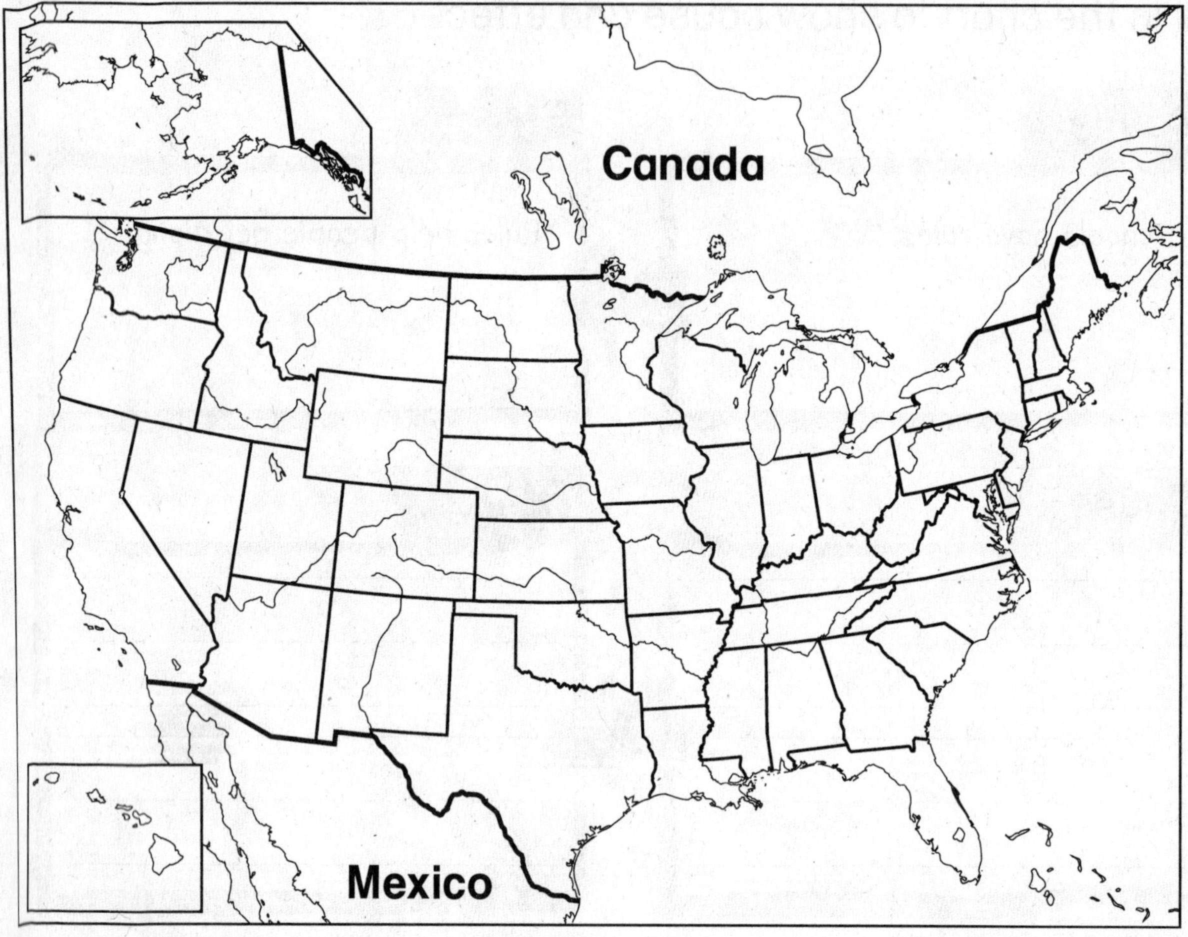

1. Color your state green.

2. Place a red dot where your community is located in your state.

3. Color the rest of your country brown.

CALIFORNIA STANDARDS HSS 1.2, 1.2.1; CS 4

Use after reading Unit 2, Lesson 1, pages 58–61.

Name ______________________ Date ________

MAP AND GLOBE SKILLS

Color a Globe

Follow the directions below the globes.

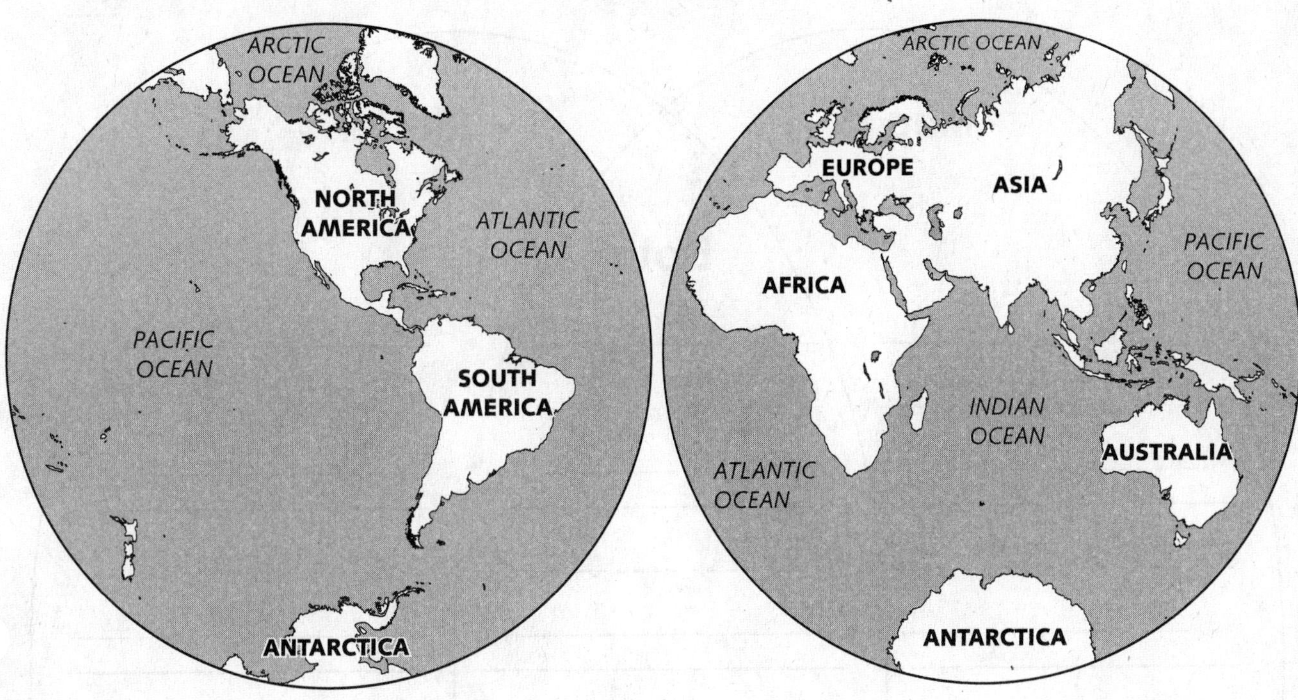

1. Find Africa. Color it green.
2. Find the continent where you live. Color it yellow.
3. Color the Atlantic Ocean blue.
4. Find Australia. Color it red.

CALIFORNIA STANDARDS HSS 1.2.1; CS 4

Use after reading Unit 2,
Skill Lesson, pages 62–63.

Name ______________________ Date __________

Compare Maps and Models

Write ways that a map and a model are alike and different.

Map

Both

Model

CALIFORNIA STANDARDS HSS 1.2.2

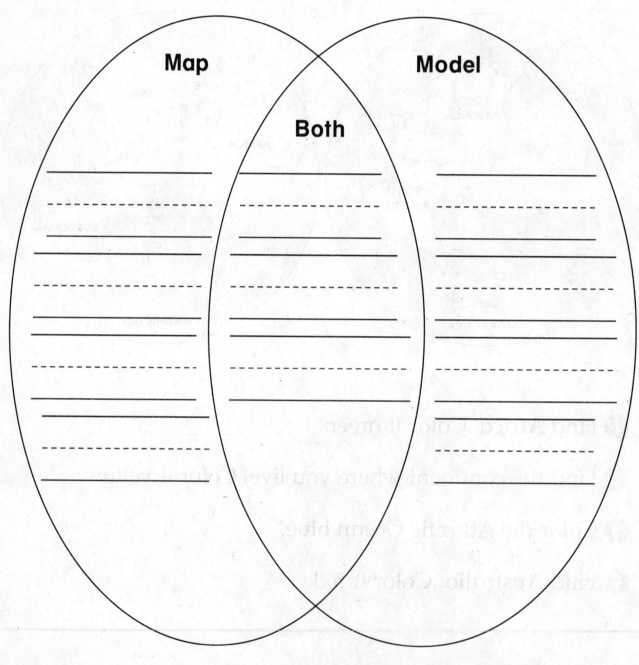

Use after reading Unit 2, Lesson 2, pages 64–67.

Name ______________________ Date __________

MAP AND GLOBE SKILLS

Mapping Symbols

Color the pictures in the map legend and on the map. Then draw a new symbol in the map legend and on the map.

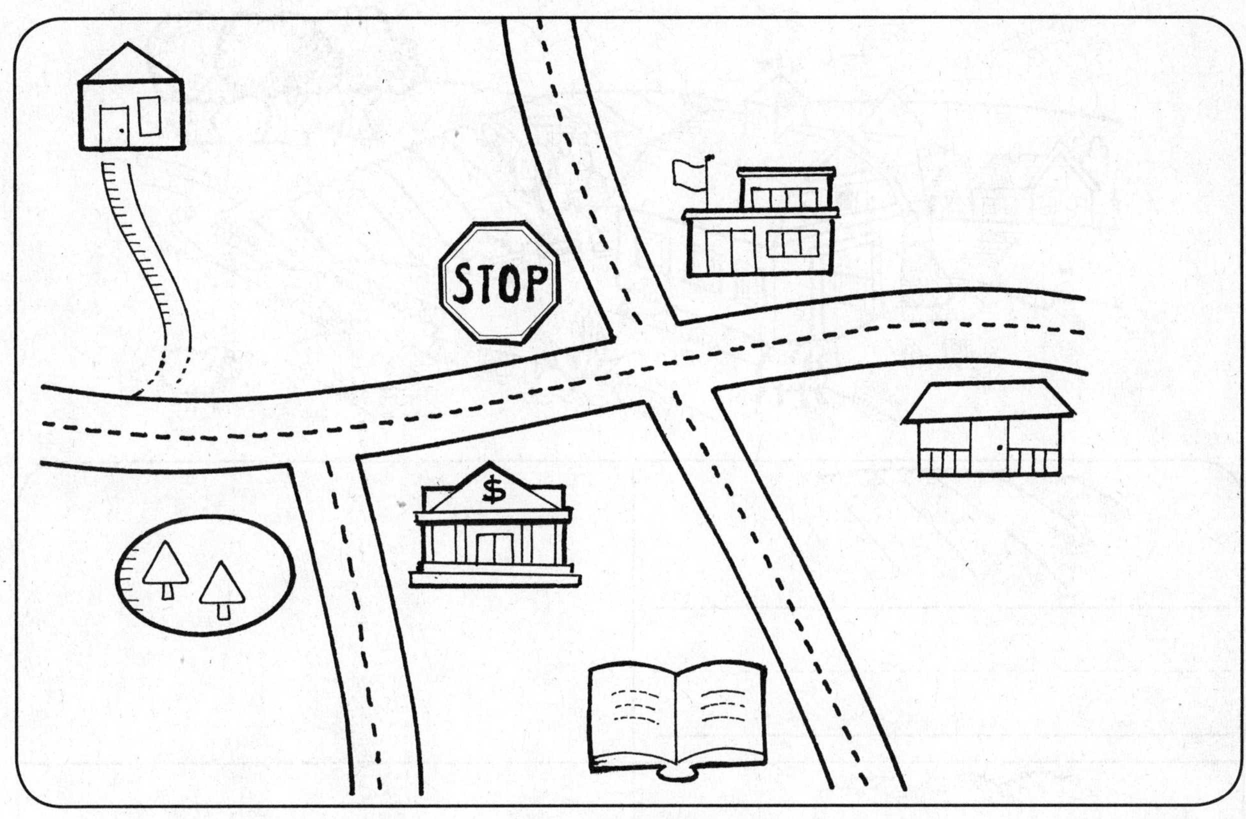

Map Legend

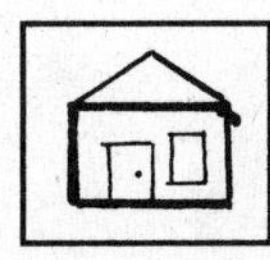
house

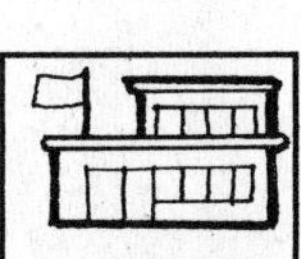
school

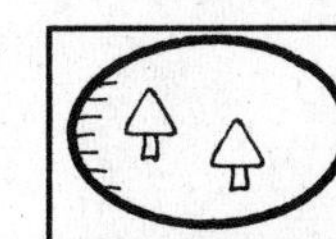
park

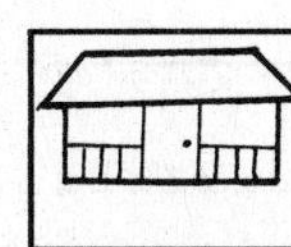
store

library

bank

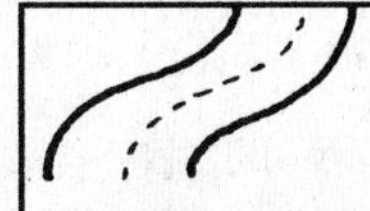
street

stop sign

hospital

CALIFORNIA STANDARDS HSS 1.2.3; CS 4

Use after reading Unit 2, Skill Lesson, pages 68–69.

Name ______________________ Date __________

Earth's Resources

Write the names of three resources you see in the picture. Draw something that comes from each resource.

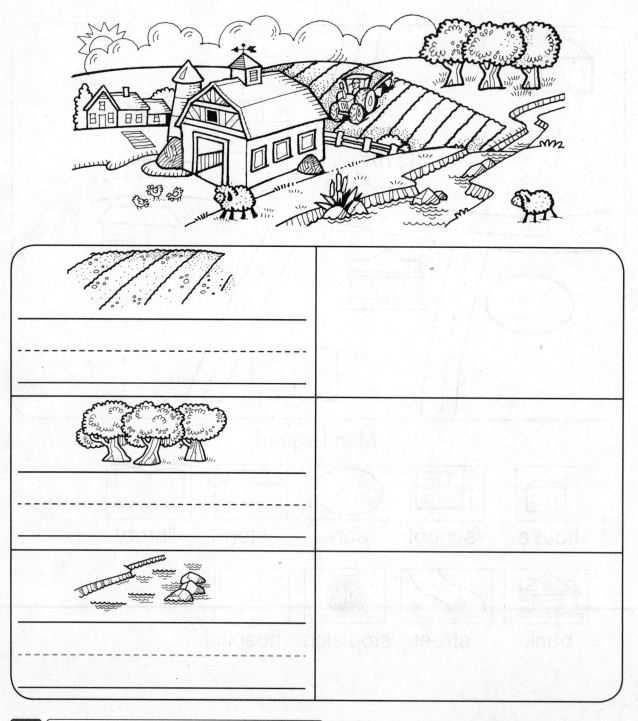

______________________	
______________________	
______________________	

CALIFORNIA STANDARDS HSS 1.2, 1.2.4; HI 2

Use after reading Unit 2, Lesson 3, pages 70–75.

Name ______________________ Date __________

MAP AND GLOBE SKILLS

Following Directions

Color the answers to the questions.

1. What is south of the pond? Color it brown.

2. What is west of the sandbox? Color it red.

3. What is north of the picnic table? Color it green.

Circle the word that tells which way to go.

4. from the garden to the pond
   north south east west

5. from the playground to the picnic table
   north south east west

 CALIFORNIA STANDARDS HSS 1.2, 1.2.3; CS 4, 5

Use after reading Unit 2, Skill Lesson, pages 76–77.

Name ________________________ Date __________

Dressing for the Weather

Write the name of the season that matches each picture. Which season is missing? Write the name of that season, and finish the picture. Be sure to draw clothing to match the weather.

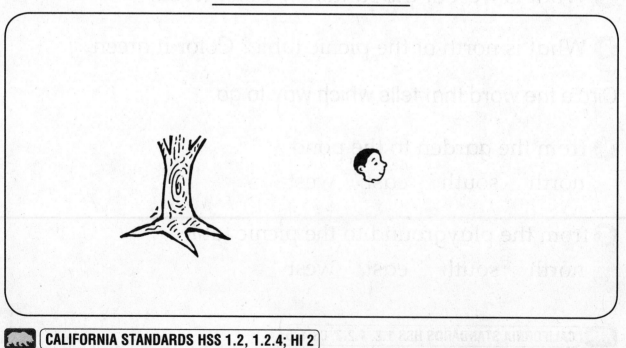

CALIFORNIA STANDARDS HSS 1.2, 1.2.4; HI 2

Use after reading Unit 2, Lesson 4, pages 80–83.

Name ______________________ Date __________

Unit 2 Study Guide

Read the letter. Use the words in the box to fill in the blanks.

states	weather	globe	border	map

Dear Sergei,

I love living in California. The ______________ is nice in every season. I love the snow and the sunshine. In California, you get both! If you want to see where I live, you can find the location of California by using a ______________ or a ______________. It shares a ______________ with Oregon, Nevada, and Arizona. They are all ______________ in the United States. What is it like where you live?

Your Pen Pal,

Penny

CALIFORNIA STANDARDS HSS 1.2, 1.2.1, 1.2.4

Use after reading Unit 2, pages 49–96.

Name ________________________ Date __________

READING SOCIAL STUDIES

Categorize and Classify

Fill in the chart to categorize and classify what you have learned.

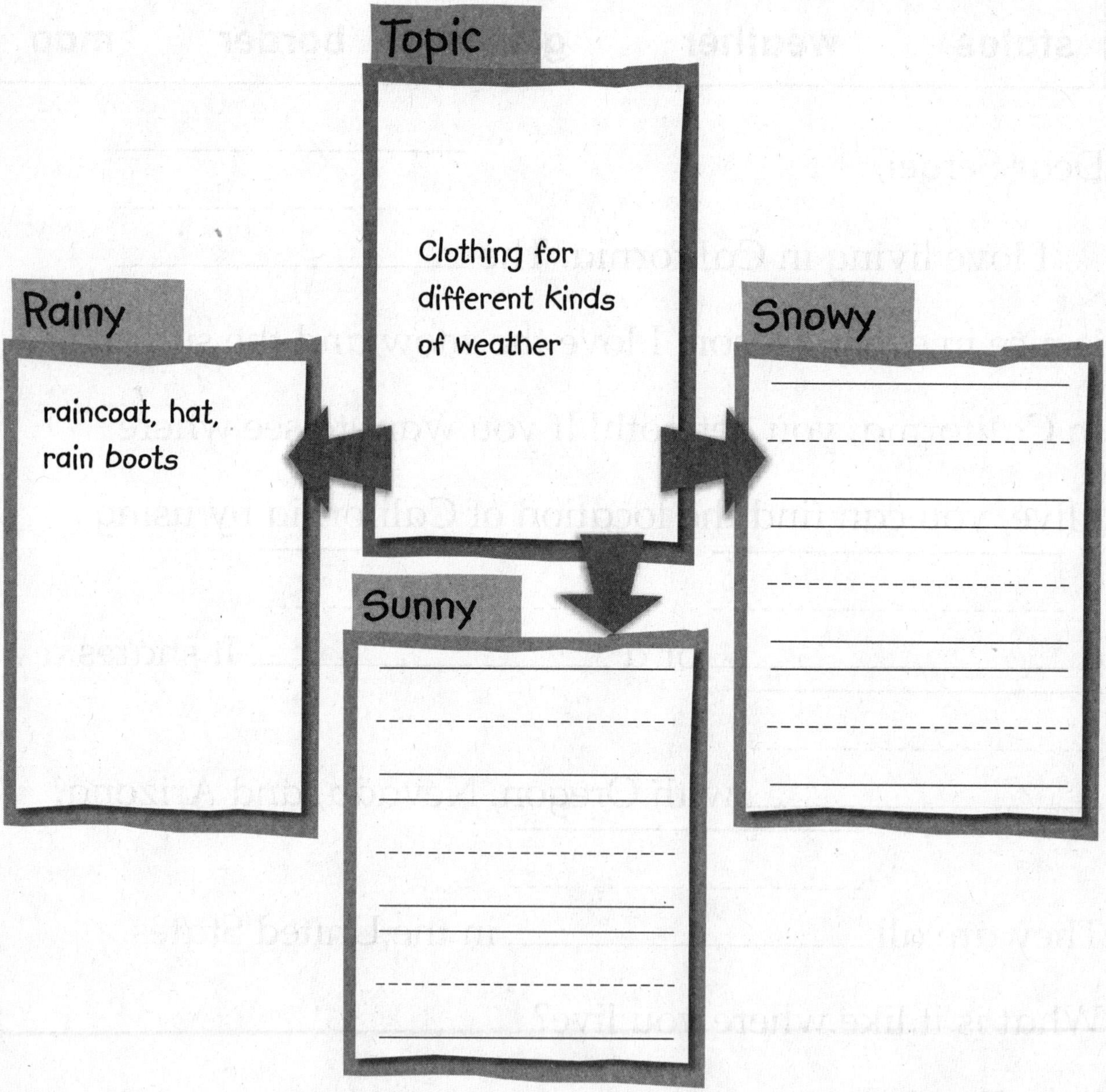

Topic

Clothing for different kinds of weather

Rainy

raincoat, hat, rain boots

Snowy

____

____

____

Sunny

____

____

____

CALIFORNIA STANDARDS HSS 1.2, 1.2.4; HI 2

Use after reading Unit 2, pages 49–96.

Name ______________________ Date __________

The Pledge

Use the words in the box to fill in the blanks.

liberty	Flag	pledge	Nation	States

I ______________ allegiance to the ______________

of the United ______________ of America, and to the

Republic for which it stands, one ______________ under

God, indivisible, with ______________ and justice

for all.

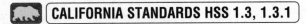

CALIFORNIA STANDARDS HSS 1.3, 1.3.1

Use after reading Unit 3, Lesson 1, pages 106–109.

Name ____________________ Date __________

National Holidays

Write the name of each holiday that matches the pictures. Finish the big picture to show how the family honors our country's flag on Flag Day.

CALIFORNIA STANDARDS HSS 1.3, 1.3.2

Use after reading Unit 3, Lesson 2, pages 112–115.

Name ______________________ Date __________

CHART AND GRAPH SKILLS

May Days

May						
Sunday	Monday	Tuesday	Wednesday	Thursday	Friday	Saturday
				1 May Day	2	3
4	5 Cinco de Mayo	6	7	8	9	10
11 Mother's Day	12	13	14	15	16	17
18	19	20	21	22	23	24
25	26 Memorial Day	27	28	29	30	31

1. What month does the calendar show? ______________________

2. On what day of the week is May Day? ______________________

3. If today is May 6, what day is tomorrow? ______________________

4. If today is May 20, what day was yesterday? ______________________

CALIFORNIA STANDARDS HSS 1.3.2; CS 2

Use after reading Unit 3,
Skill Lesson, pages 116–117.

Name ______________________ Date __________

National Symbols

Liberty Bell

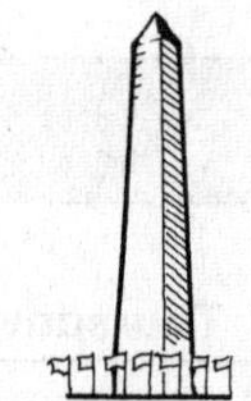

Washington Monument

Statue of Liberty

American flag

Write the name of a symbol to complete each sentence.

1. The ______________________ holds a torch.
2. The ______________________ honors our first President.
3. Each star on the ______________________ stands for a state.
4. The ______________________ stands for liberty and freedom.

CALIFORNIA STANDARDS HSS 1.3, 1.3.3

Use after reading Unit 3, Lesson 3, pages 120–123.

Name ______________________ Date __________

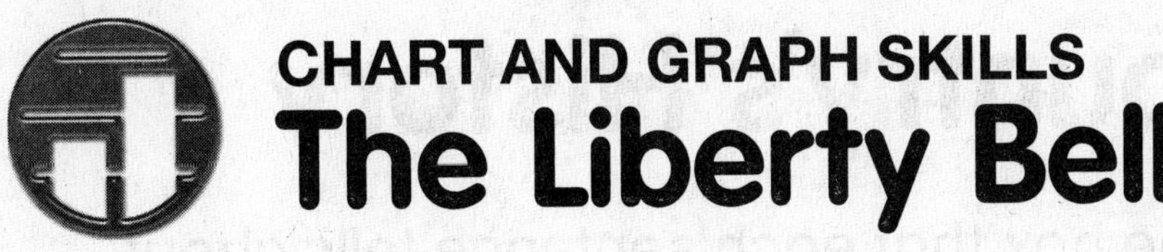

CHART AND GRAPH SKILLS

The Liberty Bell

Read the diagram to answer the questions.

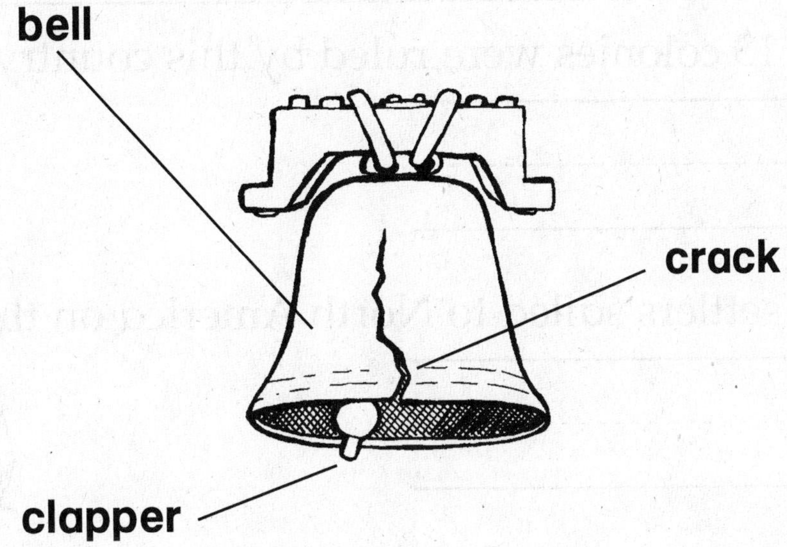

1 This is a diagram of the ______________________.

2 The part of the bell that makes the ringing sound is ______________________ called a ______________________.

3 What else do you learn about the Liberty Bell from this ______________________ diagram? ______________________

CALIFORNIA STANDARDS HSS 1.3, 1.3.3; HR 2

Use after reading Unit 3, Skill Lesson, pages 124–125.

Name ______________________ Date __________

Our Country's History

Write the word from the box that each sentence tells about.

Mayflower	Constitution	settler	England	freedom

1. The first 13 colonies were ruled by this country.

   ____

2. The first settlers sailed to North America on this ship.

   ____

3. This is someone who makes a home in a new place.

   ____

4. Americans celebrate this on Independence Day.

   ____

5. This set of rules leads our country.

   ____

CALIFORNIA STANDARDS HSS 1.3, 1.3.3; HI 1

Use after reading Unit 3, Lesson 4, pages 126–129.

Name ______________________ Date ____________

Study Guide

Read the paragraph. Use the words in the box to fill in the blanks.

hero	Pledge	landmarks	flag	freedom

Our ________________ has stars and stripes. It reminds us of the ________________ we have in our country. We show respect for the flag when we say the ________________ of Allegiance. Sometimes we fly the flag when we want to honor a ________________ for doing something brave or important. Some heroes are honored with ________________ that we can visit.

CALIFORNIA STANDARDS HSS 1.3, 1.3.2, 1.3.3

Name ______________________________ Date __________

READING SOCIAL STUDIES

Main Idea and Details

Fill in the chart to show main idea and details.

Main Idea

The Pledge of Allegiance reminds us about being good citizens.

Details

We face the flag when we say the pledge.		

CALIFORNIA STANDARDS HSS 1.3, 1.3.3

Use after reading Unit 3, pages 97–144.

Name ______________________ Date __________

School Tools Then and Now

Write then or now to tell about each object.

CALIFORNIA STANDARDS HSS 1.4, 1.4.1; CS 2

Use after reading Unit 4, Lesson 1, pages 158–163.

Name ______________________ Date __________

CHART AND GRAPH SKILLS

Which Room?

Mrs. Garza and Mr. Todd have new school supplies. Mrs. Garza teaches music. Mr. Todd teaches art.

Look at the picture. Which things go in each room? Draw pictures to complete the table.

New School Supplies	
Mrs. Garza's Room	**Mr. Todd's Room**

Use after reading Unit 4, Skill Lesson, pages 164–165.

Name ______________________________ Date __________

Changes

Look at the picture of a town of long ago. Then, draw the town the way it might look today.

CALIFORNIA STANDARDS HSS 1.4, 1.4.1; CS 3

Use after reading Unit 4, Lesson 2, pages 166–169.

Name ______________________ Date __________

CHART AND GRAPH SKILLS

Tina's Time Line

Finish the sentences to tell about Tina's time line.

 Presidents' Day– No school today!	 Library day	 My birthday	 Dentist today	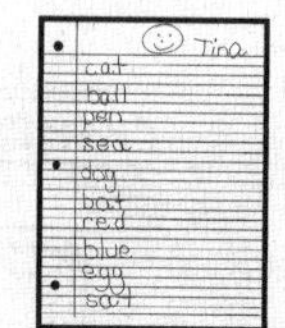 Spelling test
Monday	**Tuesday**	**Wednesday**	**Thursday**	**Friday**

1. Tina's time line shows ____________ days.
2. Tina did not go to school on ____________ because it was ____________.
3. She went to the library on ____________.
4. Tina's birthday was on ____________.
5. She saw the dentist on ____________.
6. The last thing on Tina's time line happened on ____________.

 CALIFORNIA STANDARDS HSS 1.4; CS 1

Use after reading Unit 4, Skill Lesson, pages 170–171.

Name ______________________ Date __________

Transportation Then and Now

Draw a picture of transportation from long ago or today to complete the chart.

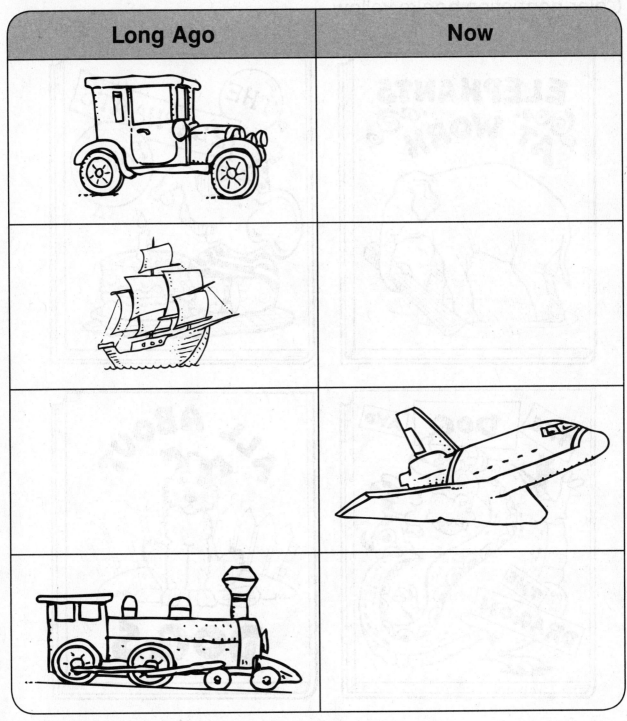

Long Ago	Now

	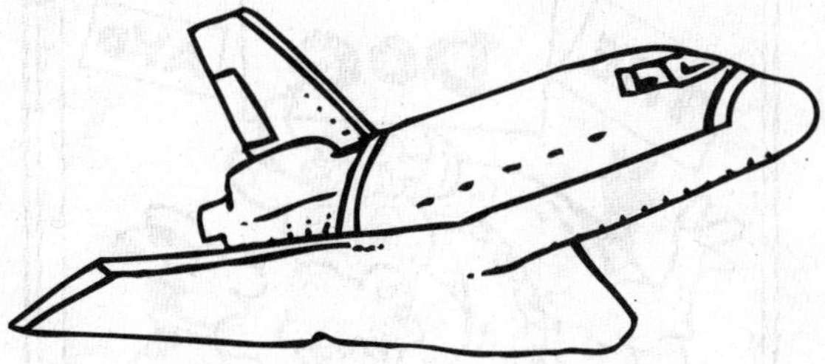

CALIFORNIA STANDARDS HSS 1.4, 1.4.2; CS 2, 3

Use after reading Unit 4, Lesson 3, pages 174–179.

Name ______________________________ Date ____________

CRITICAL THINKING SKILLS

Tell Fact from Fiction

Study the book covers. Color fiction books red.

Color nonfiction books yellow.

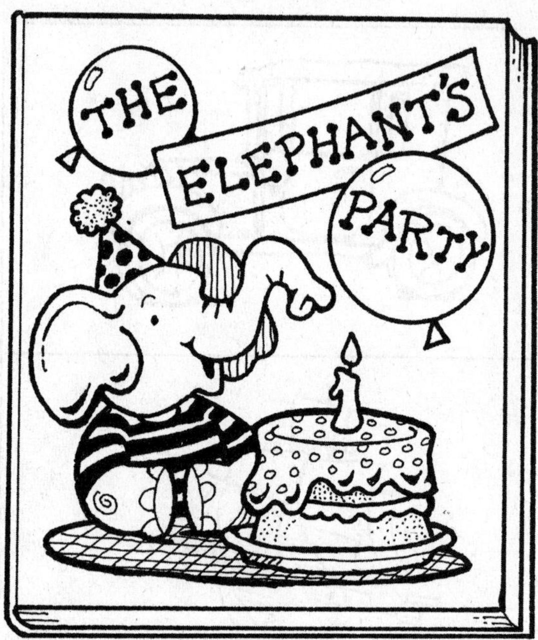

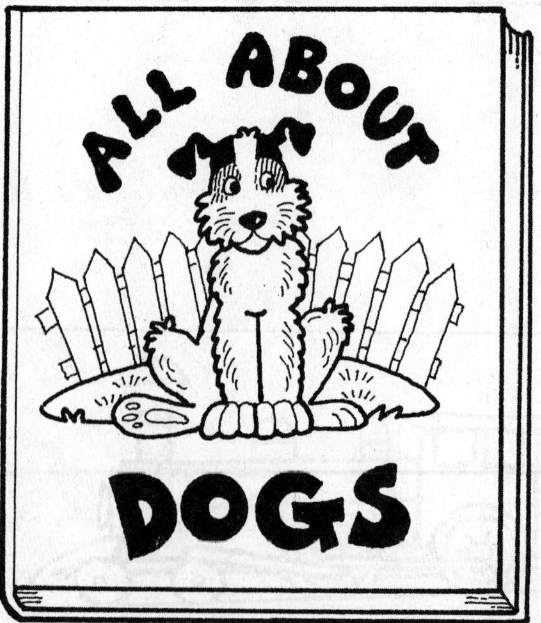

CALIFORNIA STANDARDS HSS 1.4.3; HR 3

Use after reading Unit 4, Skill Lesson, pages 180–181.

Name ______________________ Date __________

Which Came First?

Match each set to tell which item or person came first, next, and last.

1 grandson 2 grandmother 3 mom	first next last
4 e-mail 5 letters 6 phone	first next last
7 DVDs 8 drawings 9 photographs	first next last

CALIFORNIA STANDARDS HSS 1.4, 1.4.3; CS 1, 3

Use after reading Unit 4, Lesson 4, pages 184–189.

Name ______________________ Date __________

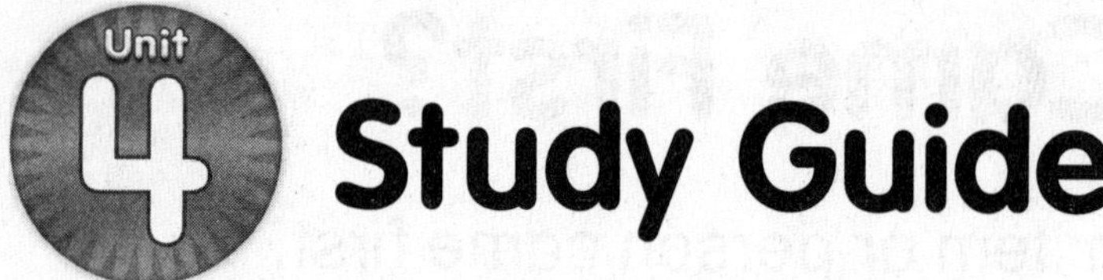

Study Guide

Read the paragraph. Use the words in the box to fill in the blanks.

technology	past	change	communication	present

Places, schools, and transportation ______________________ over time. In the ______________________, children dipped pens into ink to write. In the ______________________, we use pens or pencils. ______________________ has helped people go places faster and safer. It has also changed our ______________________, or the way we share ideas and feelings.

CALIFORNIA STANDARDS HSS 1.4, 1.4.1, 1.4.2, 1.4.3; CS 3

Use after reading Unit 4, pages 145–208.

Name ______________________ Date __________

READING SOCIAL STUDIES

Sequence

Fill in the chart to sequence what you have learned.

First	Next	Last
Transportation was very slow long ago. Many people did not travel far from home.		

CALIFORNIA STANDARDS HSS 1.4, 1.4.2; CS 1, CS 3

Use after reading Unit 4, pages 145–208.

Name ______________________ Date __________

Different People, Different Cultures

Draw pictures that show three things about your culture. Share your pictures with the class. Talk about how the pictures are alike and different.

Me

My Favorite Food

My Favorite Holiday

CALIFORNIA STANDARDS HSS 1.5, 1.5.1; HI 2

Use after reading Unit 5, Lesson I, pages 220–223.

Name ______________________ Date __________

How Did They Help?

American Indians helped early settlers who came to America. Label each picture to tell how they helped.

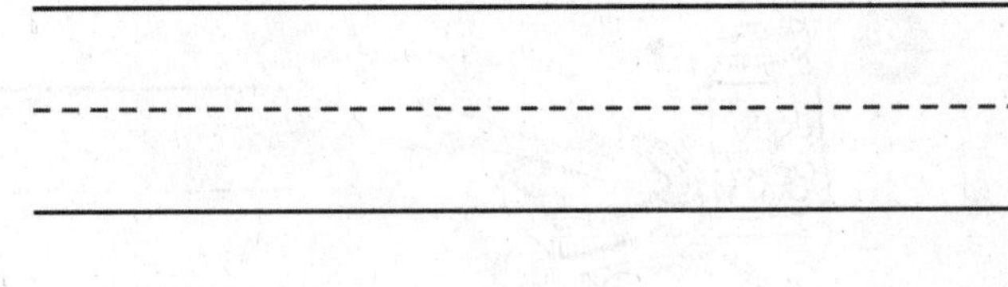

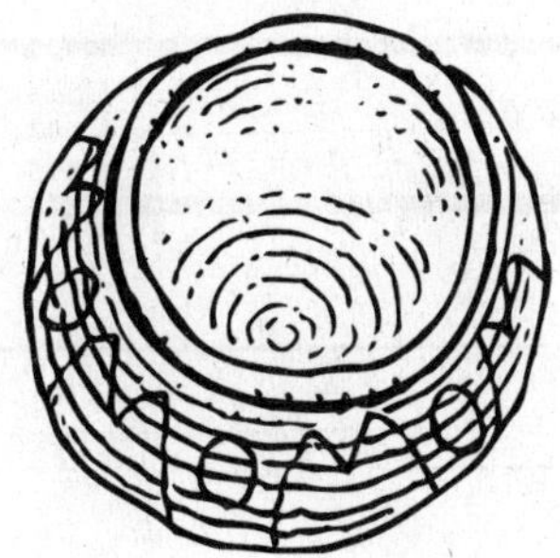

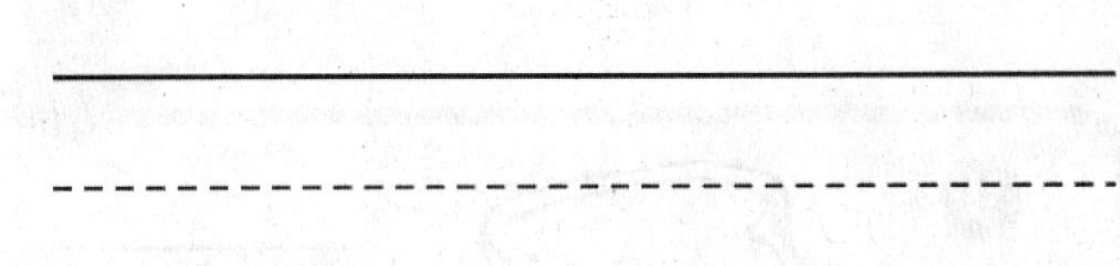

CALIFORNIA STANDARDS HSS 1.5, 1.5.2; HI 1

Use after reading Unit 5, Lesson 2, pages 226–231.

Name ______________________ Date __________

CHART AND GRAPH SKILLS

Follow a Flowchart

Label the flowchart to show how to make a peanut butter and jelly sandwich.

1 ______________________

2 ______________________

Peanut Butter

3 ______________________

Jelly

4 ______________________

Use after reading Unit 5, Skill Lesson, pages 232–233.

Name ______________________ Date __________

All About People

Finish the chart. In the last box, write one more fact you learned. In the first box, write the big idea of this lesson.

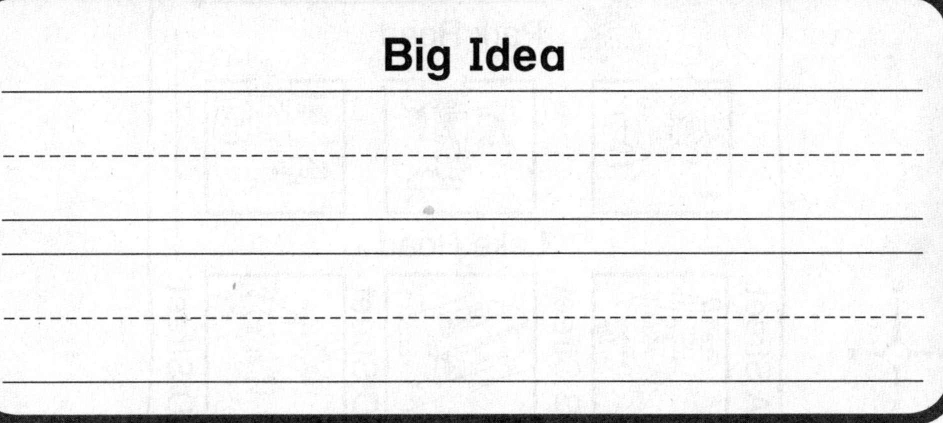

Fact
Some foods we eat were brought to this country by immigrants.

Fact
Some games we play were brought to this country by immigrants.

Fact

CALIFORNIA STANDARDS HSS 1.5, 1.5.2; HI 2

Use after reading Unit 5, Lesson 3, pages 236–241.

Name ______________________ Date __________

MAP AND GLOBE SKILLS

Mike's Route

Follow Mike's route to the library. Write north, south, east, or west to tell how to get there.

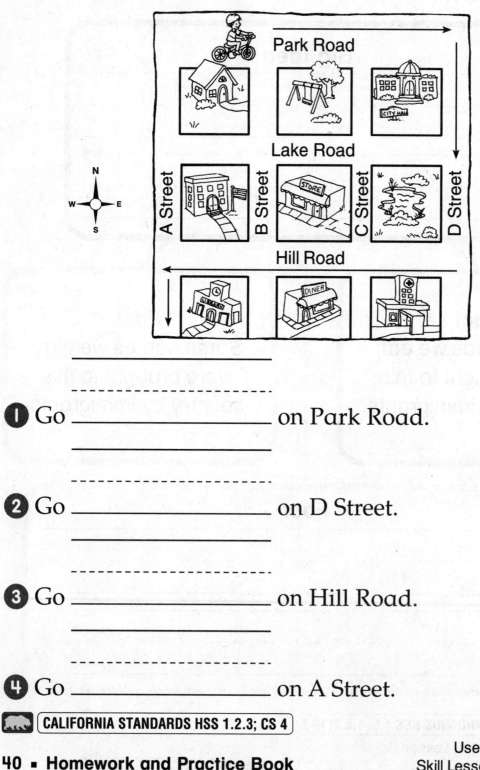

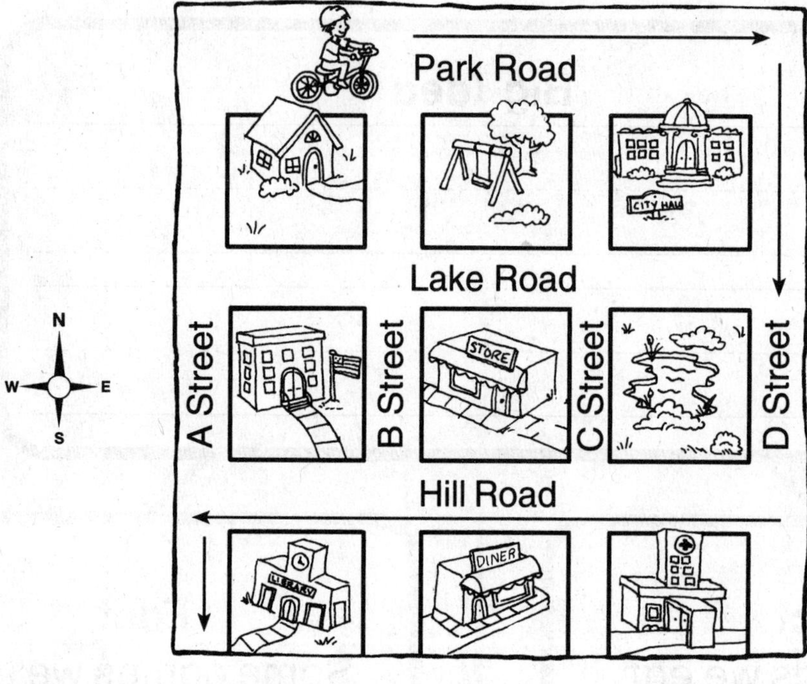

1 Go ______________________ on Park Road.

2 Go ______________________ on D Street.

3 Go ______________________ on Hill Road.

4 Go ______________________ on A Street.

CALIFORNIA STANDARDS HSS 1.2.3; CS 4

Use after reading Unit 5, Skill Lesson, pages 242–243.

Name ______________________________ Date __________

Folktales

Write the name of your favorite folktale, and write about a part of the story you like. Then draw a picture from the story. Tell a friend what happens in the folktale.

My favorite folktale is ______________________________

____.

I like the part of the story when ______________________________

____.

Here's a picture from the story:

CALIFORNIA STANDARDS HSS 1.5, 1.5.3

Use after reading Unit 5, Lesson 4, pages 244–249.

Name ______________________ Date __________

Let's Eat!

Read the sentences. Write a check mark (✓) next to the customs you share. Then write about your family's customs for meals.

In Japan, people eat their meals at a low table. They sit on pillows and eat with chopsticks. They enjoy talking with family and friends.

- ☐ sit at a table
- ☐ eat with chopsticks
- ☐ sit on pillows
- ☐ talk with family and friends

In my family, we ______________________________

____

____.

CALIFORNIA STANDARDS HSS 1.5, 1.5.3; HI 2

Use after reading Unit 5, Lesson 5, pages 250–253.

Name ______________________ Date __________

Unit 5 Study Guide

Read the paragraph. Use the words in the box to fill in the blanks.

culture	immigrants	traditions	history	folktales

We can learn about a group's way of life by studying its ______________. All people have ______________, or special ways of doing things that are passed from parents to children. ______________ is the story of what has happened in the past. Many people share their history by telling ______________, or stories passed from person to person. When ______________ come to our country to start a new life, they have stories to tell, too.

CALIFORNIA STANDARDS HSS 1.5, 1.5.1, 1.5.2, 1.5.3

Name ______________________ Date __________

READING SOCIAL STUDIES

Compare and Contrast

Fill in the chart to compare and contrast things you have learned.

American Indians	Similar	Immigrants
		Came to America looking for a new home

Name ______________________________ Date __________

Pet Shopping List

Read the list. Circle in blue the words that name services. Circle in red the words that name goods. Then answer the questions.

List
take dog to vet
take dog for grooming
get dog food
get new leash
get toy

What are two other goods that might be needed for a pet?

____

____

What is one other service that might be needed for a pet?

____

____

CALIFORNIA STANDARDS HSS 1.6, 1.6.1

Use after reading Unit 6,
Lesson 1, pages 276–279.

Name ______________________ Date __________

CHART AND GRAPH SKILLS

Make a Picture Graph

Ask five friends to choose the sport they like best. Draw a sneaker next to a sport each time a friend chooses it. Then answer the questions.

We Like Sports	
(football)	
(basketball)	
(baseball)	
(soccer)	
(hockey)	

Legend:  = one person

The sport chosen the most is ______________________.

The sport chosen the least is ______________________.

Use after reading Unit 6, Skill Lesson, pages 280–281.

Name ______________________ Date ____________

Work Chat

Finish the cartoon. Write an answer each person might give.

1. ______________________

Why do you volunteer at the library?

2. ______________________

Why will you work someday?

What kind of work will you do?

3. ______________________

CALIFORNIA STANDARDS HSS 1.6, 1.6.2

Use after reading Unit 6, Lesson 2, pages 282–287.

Name ______________________ Date __________

Buy, Sell, and Save

Choose a sentence from the box to tell about each picture.

Sellers save some of their money.
Sellers sell goods to earn money.
Sellers buy things they need.

1 ______________________________

2 ______________________________

3 ______________________________

CALIFORNIA STANDARDS HSS 1.6, 1.6.1

Use after reading Unit 6, Lesson 3, pages 292–297.

Name ______________________ Date __________

CRITICAL THINKING SKILLS

Make a Choice When Buying

Lisa wants to buy a birthday present for her mom. Color the things you think she should buy. Then tell why you made your choices.

> I have $20.
>
> I want to buy a gift, a card, and wrapping paper.

____

____

CALIFORNIA STANDARDS HSS 1.6, 1.6.1; HI 4

Use after reading Unit 6, Skill Lesson, pages 298–299.

Name ______________________ Date __________

Pencil Factory

Number the pictures to show the order of steps in making pencils. Then complete the sentence.

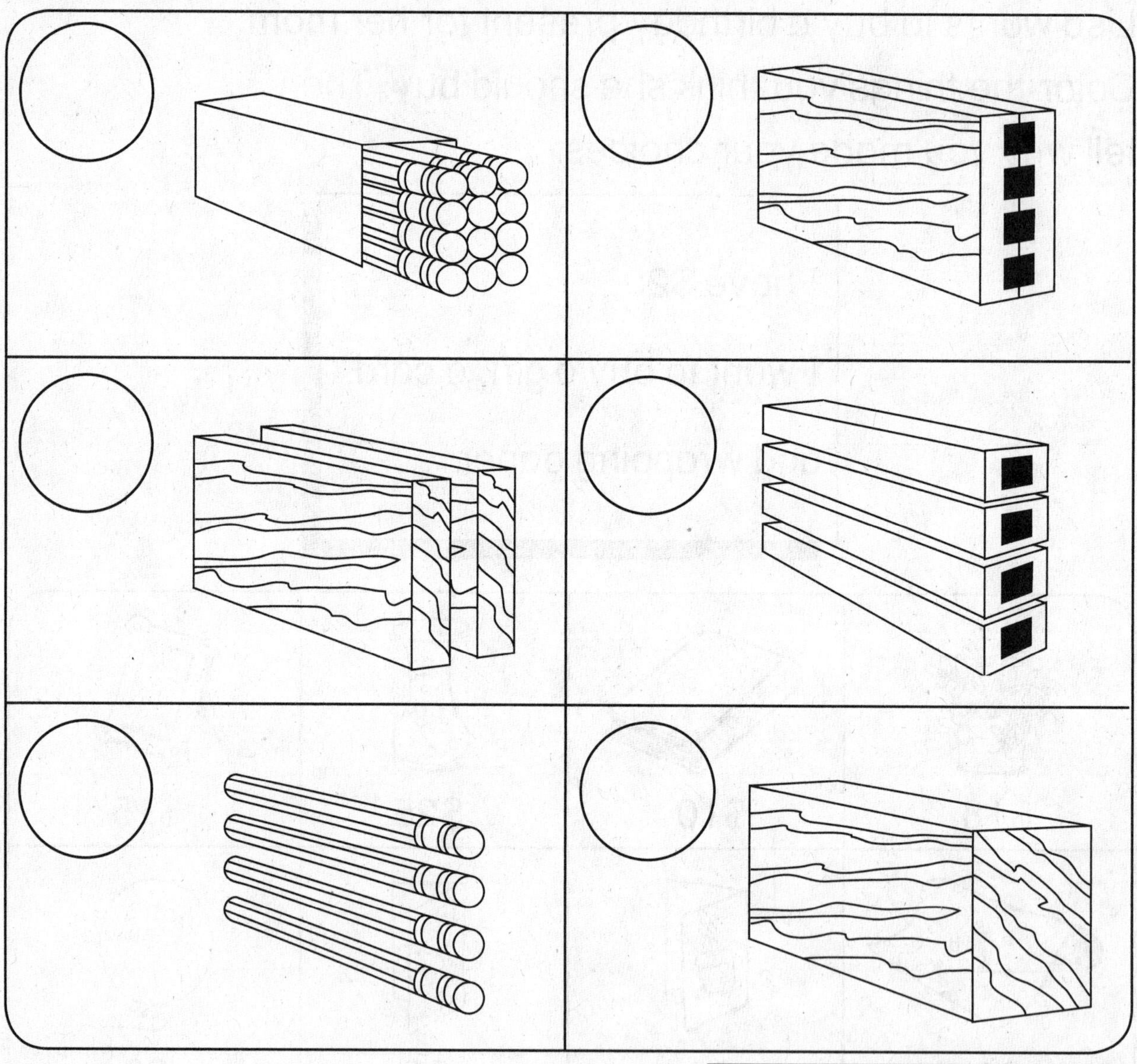

To make pencils, people in a factory ______________________

____

CALIFORNIA STANDARDS HSS 1.6, 1.6.2

Use after reading Unit 6, Lesson 4, pages 300–305.

Name ______________________________ Date __________

CHART AND GRAPH SKILLS

Make a Bar Graph

Ask five friends to choose their favorite food from the pictures on the graph. Color in one space by a food each time someone chooses it. Then use the graph to finish the sentences.

	0	1	2	3	4	5

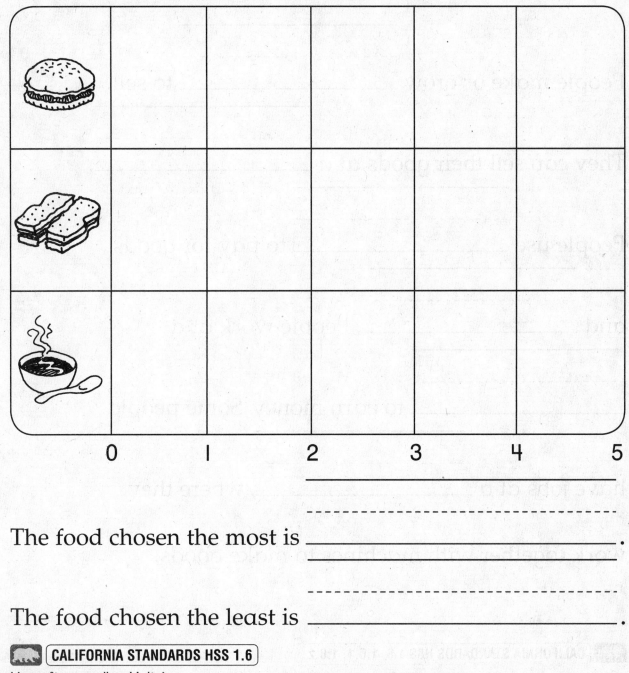

The food chosen the most is ______________________.

The food chosen the least is ______________________.

 CALIFORNIA STANDARDS HSS 1.6

Use after reading Unit 6, Skill Lesson, pages 306–307.

Name ______________________ Date __________

Study Guide

Read the paragraph. Use the words in the box to fill in the blanks.

services	money	market	factory	goods	job

People make or grow ______________ to sell. They can sell their goods at a ______________. People use ______________ to pay for goods and ______________. People work at a ______________ to earn money. Some people have jobs at a ______________, where they work together with machines to make goods.

CALIFORNIA STANDARDS HSS 1.6, 1.6.1, 1.6.2

 Use after reading Unit 6, pages 265–320.

Name ______________________ Date __________

READING SOCIAL STUDIES

Recall and Retell

Fill in the chart to recall and retell what you have learned.

Recall Detail	Retell
People make and sell goods and sell services.	

Recall Detail

Recall Detail

CALIFORNIA STANDARDS HSS 1.6, 1.6.1, 1.6.2

Use after reading Unit 6, pages 265–320.